Creative Confidence
Ignite Your Inner Artist

Table of Contents

Chapter 1. Introduction

Uncover your artistic flair with our comprehensive Special Report on 'Creative Confidence: Ignite Your Inner Artist.' This engaging guide is not just a report - it's a journey towards the unexplored domains of your creative potential, armed with techniques that drive world-class artists! Whether you're looking to paint a masterpiece, pen a captivating poem, design an innovative product, or simply add a little more color to your life, we've got you covered. The report is composed of thought-provoking insights, booster techniques, and inspiring anecdotes that aim to awaken the dormant creative spirits in you. Eager to get your creative juices flowing? Brighten up your world and embark on an exciting, creative journey with this special report. Let your canvas be the world and your paintbrush, unbridled imagination. It's time to dream, create and inspire like never before! Ready to meet the artist within? Join us—this special report could be the key to unlock your artistic prowess.

Chapter 2. Unleashing Your Inner Artist

"Imagine a door. Beyond that door lies a universe brimming with endless possibilities, expressive freedoms, and the unchecked power of creation. You hold the key to that door, and we are about to venture into unlocking it. Unleashing your inner artist begins with embracing and understanding the innate creativity that resides within you.

2.1. Embrace Your Innate Creative Potentials

Every individual, regardless of experience or profession, possesses an intrinsic creative capability. According to an IBM study, creativity is listed as the most crucial leadership quality, even higher than integrity or vision. Indeed, it is our creative potential that can ignite innovation in even the most traditional industries.

But to harness this potential, we must first acknowledge and embrace it. Strive to see the world not for what it is, but what it could be. Infuse creativity into everyday life – paint not just with the colors on a canvas, but also with the words you use, the thoughts you think, and the actions you take. Once you have accepted this vital perspective shift, the path to artistic expression becomes clearer, paving the way for you to actualize the artist residing within.

2.2. Sharpen Your Artistic Observation

A keen sense of observation is an artist's first and foremost tool. Artists view the world differently, with a heightened level of

Environmental Perception, or 'E.P.' This term, coined by Dr. Albert More, refers to an increased awareness of the minutiae existing in our environment.

E.P. involves patience, curiosity, and profound attention to detail, allowing you to see beyond the surface and perceive the intricate details of everyday life. It might be the interplay of light and shadow in a busy street, the juxtaposition of colors in a sunset, or the emotional depth in a simple conversation. Practicing this deeper level of observation nurtures your artistic insight, thereby enriching your creative reservoir.

2.3. Cultivate an Artistic Mindset

Developing an artistic mindset doesn't necessarily mean you have to create artwork—it's about creating your world. It's about grooming a particular kind of consciousness steeped in creativity, innovation, and whimsical imagination.

To nurture this mindset, initiate an in-depth exploration of varied art forms. Study the works of master artists, delve into different artistic styles and genres, understand the power of color, composition, light, and form. But most importantly, remember that the world is your canvas and you are its painter. Don't be timid in experimenting with new ideas or approaches—it is in creative blunders that true innovations are often found.

2.4. Implement Creative Practices

Creativity is like a muscle—it needs to be continually worked upon and strengthened. To unlock your inner potential, design and implement a creativity workout regime. This could involve daily art practices like painting, sketching, or writing; it could also be a mindful activity such as a contemplative walk or meditative practice focused on nourishing your creative spirit.

For your creative workouts, identify a quiet, inspiring space where you're free to express without inhibitions. Surround yourself with artworks or objects that move or inspire you. Allocate a set time for these practices and incorporate them into your daily routine.

2.5. Develop Resilience and Perseverance

Do not fear failure—view it as a stepping stone towards mastery. The path to creative enlightenment is strewn with hurdles and hardships, but it is these trials that refine your artistic spirit. Embrace criticism and learn from it, for it helps in the transformation of your art. Remember, failure is just a springboard for coming up with something even better—it's not the end of your creativity but the igniting spark.

2.6. Find Your Unique Artistic Voice

Finally, amidst the vast seas of artistic styles and methods, find your unique artistic voice. Understand that your artistic expression is an extension of yourself—it is your thoughts, emotions, experiences, and perspectives translated into art. Celebrate your individuality, and let your authenticity shine through your creative pursuits.

This journey towards uncovering your inner artist promises to be rewarding, filled with revelations and self-discovery. Remember, there isn't a definitive set path or 'correct way' to be an artist. Your journey is unique—it's a passage of constant learning, experimenting, and evolving. As Picasso rightfully said, 'Every child is an artist. The problem is how to remain an artist once we grow up.'

Embrace your creative spirit, continually nurture and refine it, and you are sure to uncover the artist within you, ready to paint your life with vibrant colors of creativity and expression."

Chapter 3. Fostering a Creative Mindset

Having a creative mindset is not a trait reserved for the select few. It is, in fact, an innate human quality—a natural way of thinking that can be nurtured, developed, and harnessed by anyone. It's akin to embarking on a lifelong journey of discovery, exploration, and imaginative expression.

3.1. Cultivating Curiosity

Curiosity is the catalyst that triggers creativity. It's that little spark that ignites a bonfire of ideas, urging you to challenge the status quo and explore new perspectives. To nurture curiosity, think like a child. Have the desire to understand, question everything, and never stop learning.

Adopt the 'What if' approach, wondering about the possible alternatives and outcomes. Challenge conventional wisdom, defy the norm, and embrace the journey of questioning. It is through this relentless quest that creative solutions are born.

3.2. Embracing Playfulness

Remember how, as children, we used to invent games, make up stories, and imagine incredible worlds? That wasn't just play; it was the art of creativity. Embracing playfulness as adults can lead to fewer self-imposed restrictions and more innovative ideas.

Creativity flourishes in a stress-free environment. Therefore, strive to cultivate an environment where creativity can thrive—whether that's surrounding yourself with inspiring art, going on frequent nature walks, or simply dedicating "playtime" to explore new hobbies or interests.

3.3. Overcoming Fear of Failure

Fear is one of the most inhibiting factors of creativity. A fear of failure, judgment, or criticism can restrain you from exploring and expressing original ideas. Embrace failure as an inevitable component of success. It's essential to understand that failure is not the opposite of success but part of its process.

Moreover, view failure as a learning curve rather than a setback. Make 'fail fast and improve' your mantra and remember, every great piece of art, was once, a work-in-progress.

3.4. Developing Observational Skills

A creative mind always remains attentive to its environment, continuously observing and absorbing stimuli. It's a perpetual process of learning and understanding that makes you see the ordinary in an extraordinary way.

Develop keen observation skills by slowing down and being fully present. Engage fully with your surroundings—notice the subtle sounds, the varying hues of colors or the intricate patterns. This way, you will see inspiration everywhere.

3.5. Encouraging Divergent Thinking

Divergent thinking is the ability to generate a wide range of ideas from a single starting point. It's a crucial component of a creative mindset, and it can be cultivated.

Promote divergent thinking by exposing yourself to various

experiences. Break habitual thinking patterns, brainstorm and encourage thoughts without judgment. The goal here is quantity over quality—at this stage, there is no such thing as a 'bad idea.'

3.6. Incorporating Mindfulness in Creativity

Mindfulness and creativity go hand in hand. When you practice mindfulness, you are fully engaged in the present moment. This lets your mind wander freely, making connections that your consciousness might overlook.

Whether it's through meditation, yoga, or simply paying attention to your breathing, mindfulness has a way of clearing the mental clutter, paving the way for creativity to flourish.

3.7. Adopting Structured Daydreaming

Scientific studies suggest that daydreaming enhances creativity. However, aimless daydreaming can lead to a loss of productivity. The solution? Structured daydreaming.

Designate specific time for daydreaming. Visualize challenges or problems during this period and let your mind wander to seek solutions. This process marries creativity with productivity.

3.8. Investing in Continual Learning

Continual learning fuels creativity. It broadens your perspective and provides a richer inventory of knowledge which acts as the raw material for creativity.

Pursue a diverse range of subjects—not just related to your field of work. Read widely, learn new languages, explore different cultures. Broadening your horizons in this way can enhance your associative thinking, leading to increased creativity.

Innovative ideas tend not to come up out of nowhere; they are often the product of connecting different pieces of information in new ways.

The journey towards fostering a creative mindset takes time and patiently consistent effort. You will encounter setbacks along the way. But remember, creativity, like any other skill, is a muscle—it grows stronger the more you use it. Let this be your guiding torch as you delve deeper into your creative journey.

Chapter 4. Roadblocks to Creativity and Overcoming Them

Creativity is an innate human trait that is uniquely personal, endlessly diverse, and endlessly elusive. This elusive quality often leads to perceived roadblocks and deterrents, which can stifle the creative process before it's even begun. Identifying, understanding, and overcoming these obstacles are essential steps in unlocking your creative potential.

The first daunting roadblock many encounter is the fear of judgement. We all are worried about what others may think or say about our creative outputs. This fear often hampers our ability to express ourselves freely and inhibits our creative instincts. However, fear and anxiety are simply manifestations of our mind, with no real substance or power. They can be overcome by taking the risk to put our work out there and open up to criticism. In vulnerability lies immense strength. It encourages empathy, fosters growth and helps shatter the draconian prism of perfectionism.

4.1. Embrace Imperfection

Art isn't synonymous with perfection. Rather, it is an expression of human emotion, an exploration of the self, and an engagement with the world. Embrace mistakes as an indispensable part of the creative process. Reframe how you perceive errors. Mistakes, instead of being indicators of failure, should be viewed as stepping stones leading towards improvement. Missteps and blunders can lead to novel ideas and unexpected avenues of creativity. A wrong brushstroke can lead to a unique texture in your painting; a flawed note can pave the way to an original melody.

The second major roadblock is lack of inspiration. Creatives often fall victim to the misconception that inspiration is a random, elusive entity that either strikes or doesn't. However, waiting for inspiration to strike is like waiting for the rain in a drought. It's better to build your well, and for that, you have to dig deep inside.

4.2. Cultivating Inspiration

Inspiration is less of an external event and more of an internal process. It's about learning to tune into your innermost thoughts, emotions, and experiences. To nurture it, indulge in a wide range of experiences, broaden your perspective by reading widely, engage in meaningful conversations, or simply take a stroll in nature. Carry a notebook with you to jot down random thoughts, fleeting ideas or even a peculiar pattern you noticed on the roadside. This routine helps incubate ideas, keeping your creative wellspring primed at all times.

Stagnation forms the third stumbling block to our creativity. Stagnant waters breed mosquitoes, and stagnant minds breed doubt. Complacency breeds creative inertia.

4.3. Creative Fluidity

To maintain creative fluidity, it is necessary to keep learning. New knowledge can be a rich source of inspiration, encouraging us to see things from a fresh perspective. Challenge the status quo, ask provocative questions and disrupt patterns to stimulate your innovative dexterity. Another great way is engaging in 'creative cross-training,' that is, learning and practicing an art form different from your usual medium. This cross-exposure invigorates your mind, boosting lateral thinking and stimulating fresh neuronal connections, leading to innovative ideas.

The fourth barrier revolves around limiting beliefs—those we adopt from the society we live in, and those we impose upon ourselves. We often undervalue our creative worth, comparing our work with others, deeming it unworthy.

4.4. Shattering Limiting Beliefs

To shatter limiting beliefs, we need to challenge and confront them. Remember that creativity is an inherently subjective process. There isn't a universal benchmark to determine its value. The joy and fulfilment you derive from the creative process holds intrinsic value, independent of external validation. Lastly, engage in self-affirmation. Remind yourself of your unique abilities and past successes. Regular reflection helps build resilience, aiding in banishing self-doubt.

Lastly, many creatives get trapped in the mighty throes of procrastination. The irony is, procrastination isn't born of laziness but rather a defense mechanism against fear—the fear of inadequacy, the fear of failure.

4.5. Overcoming Procrastination

The best antidote to procrastination is action. Start with small steps. It could be as simple as setting up your workstation, choosing your tools, or jotting down a few possible ideas. Setting up manageable daily goals works wonders. By balancing your tasks, you minimize the risk of feeling overwhelmed and steer clear of procrastination.

Unleashing creativity is not a linear journey; it's a labyrinth of self-discovery, fraught with dead ends, wrong turns, yet filled with unexpected treasures. By identifying and addressing these roadblocks, and embracing a mindset of continuous learning and growth, the elusive Muse of Creativity can indeed become a cherished friend and guide. And in this lies the unique magic of creative confidence.

Chapter 5. Understanding and Boosting Creative Confidence

Creative confidence is the belief in your ability to create change in the world around you. It is the conviction that you can achieve what you set out to do. It is a quality admired and valued not just in artists, but in people from all walks of life. It is something that can be nurtured and developed, regardless of whether one considers oneself an artist. Let's look at how to understand and boost this vital asset.

Creative confidence has its roots in four main components: attitude, knowledge, thinking style, and motivation. These elements are intrinsically intertwined and often interdependent. To foster creative confidence, one must cultivate each of these areas.

5.1. The Attitude for Creativity

Scientists and advocates of positive psychology often cite the attitude as the pivotal point for creative action. It is the way we perceive and interact with our world that defines our creative output. Therefore, it's crucial to adopt an attitude that embraces new challenges and is open to the unknown.

A growth mindset, coined by psychologist Carol Dweck, is key here. A person with a growth mindset views skills and abilities as qualities that can be developed over time. This mindset advocates that effort, rather than innate talent alone, leads to success and growth. Embrace the tenants of a growth mindset to fuel your creative confidence:

1. Foster flexibility: View challenges not as roadblocks, but as opportunities for growth. Find new solutions, knowing that risking failure is always a part of the creative journey.

2. Be patient: Recognize that creativity doesn't work on a fixed schedule or timeline. Embrace the process no matter how long it takes, cherishing the small victories along the way.

3. Embrace failure: Understand that failure is an integral part of the creative process. Each failure brings a valuable lesson that can be used to enhance future creative ventures.

5.2. Knowledge as the Foundation

Acquiring knowledge about different subjects can play a significant role in boosting creative confidence. This knowledge will serve as the foundation upon which your creative ideas will be built. Consider the following points:

1. Continual Learning: To fuel creativity, one should have an insatiable curiosity and a commitment to never-ending learning. Read extensively, explore different subjects, and never stop asking questions.

2. Practical Application: Try to apply what you learn in real-life scenarios. Learning in the classroom or from books is great, but when you use your knowledge practically, it deepens your understanding and boosts creative confidence.

3. Cross-pollination of Ideas: Learning about a wide variety of topics allows for the 'cross-pollination' of ideas. This kind of interdisciplinary learning can result in remarkable and innovative ideas, something Steve Jobs famously promoted when discussing the genesis of his innovative product designs.

5.3. Embracing Divergent Thinking

Divergent thinking, a thought process or method used to generate creative ideas by exploring many possible solutions, is another key to boosting creative confidence. Here are encouraged to discover multiple answers, rather than just one.

1. Cultivate Open-mindedness: Become comfortable with uncertainty. People who can hold multiple perspectives in their minds are typically more creative.

2. Brainstorming: Make use of brainstorming sessions to generate a pool of ideas. Remember, no idea is a bad idea in this stage. The goal is to encourage free thinking.

3. Challenging Assumptions: Regularly challenge your own assumptions about how things should be. Ask yourself: Why is this this way? Could it be different or even better?

5.4. Motivation Matters

Internal motivation can drive creative confidence. It is essential to understand what drives you and use that as fuel for your creative work.

1. Find your why: This is your internal driver, the reason you do what you do. When you understand it, it can serve as the guiding force in your creative endeavors.

2. Intrinsic vs. Extrinsic motivation: Intrinsic motivation, the drive coming from within, often leads to creativity more than extrinsic motivation, the drive based on external rewards. Learn to foster your own internal motivations for creativity.

3. Celebrate Small Wins: Each step in the right direction fuels your motivation. Recognize these small wins and let them propel you forward.

In conclusion, understanding and boosting creative confidence is an ongoing journey, not a destination. It involves a combination of cultivating the right attitude, investing in knowledge, developing the skill of divergent thinking, and understanding your own motivation. With these building blocks, you will be poised to ignite your inner artist, whatever form that might take. Now go forth and let your creativity shine!

Chapter 6. Tools and Techniques to Stimulate Your Creativity

Creativity is highly personal and largely intangible. Yet, it can also be cultivated, guided, and stimulated using a variety of practical tools and techniques. Categories range from physical items like sketchbooks or software apps to cognitive strategies or practices that stretch your thinking and open your mind to new possibilities. For the purpose of this guide, we'll explore both tangible and intangible tools and techniques that, if consistently used, can enhance your creative confidence and ignite your artistic flair.

6.1. Physical Tools

A painter's brush, a musician's instrument, a writer's notebook; all these are essential tools for expression yet also act as inspirations. It's important to find the correct tools that suit your style, assist your thinking and fit in with your comfort zone.

Notebooks: The humble notebook can be a powerful tool for capturing thoughts, ideas, doodles, and more. A preferred tool for writers, artists, and thinkers alike, the notebook's value lies in its simplicity. Sketch, write, stick, paint; it's an unobtrusive friend that allows for free flow of thoughts without limitations.

Digital Tools: Numerous digital tools and apps are available today, enabling creativity at your fingertips. Tools like Adobe Creative Suite, Canva or Procreate for artists, or Evernote and Microsoft OneNote for writers and thinkers, help in creating, collecting and organizing your thoughts and ideas. Exploring digital terrain can widen your creative landscape and cater to your varying artistic needs.

Mixed Media: From paints, markers, and charcoal—to clay, wood, or found items, mixed media offers a sensory-driven exploration that can free unconscious ideas. Physical interaction with diverse materials often inspires unique solutions and unexpected artistic outcomes.

6.2. Mental and Psychological Tools

Beyond the physical, creativity requires keen mental and psychological tools. They serve as the underpinning of your artistic journey, assisting in observing, contemplating and reflecting, essential to creative perception.

Curiosity and Observation: Cultivate an interest in the world around you. Enhance your observation skills. This tool urges you to question, explore, and delve deeper. It builds a reservoir of ideas, experiences, and insights which is a key source for original creative works. Regularly practicing mindful observation improves the quality of your creative thoughts.

Meditation: Artists have long noted the benefits of a calm and clear mind. Practicing regular meditation can help manage the distractions and stresses that block creative flow. Moreover, it promotes divergent thinking—an essential factor in creative work.

Embrace Uncertainty: Uncertainty often fuels creativity. A safe space where wild ideas can roam free, allowing for risk-taking without fear of judgment, significantly enhances creative efforts. Fostering a comfortable relationship with uncertainty can markedly boost innovation and creative self-expression.

6.3. Technique Stimulators

Techniques and practices can stimulate your creative thinking, encouraging you to break out of established patterns and discover fresh ideas.

Brainstorming: Brainstorming, as a free-thinking, non-linear process, encourages unbridled generation of ideas and possible solutions. It incites spontaneous connections, facilitates group synergy, and pushes boundaries set by critical thinking.

Mind Maps: Mind maps visually organize information, helping your brain to comprehend and remember better. The radiant structure of mind maps incites a more natural, neural network-like method of thinking, stimulating creative connections.

Free Writing: This technique involves continuous writing for a set period, without worrying about grammar, typos, or even making sense. It's a useful tool for overcoming writer's block or tapping into subconscious thoughts.

SCAMPER: This acronym stands for Substitute, Combine, Adapt, Modify, Put to another use, Eliminate and Reverse. It prompts us to ask specific questions related to each of these action words to generate novel ideas or reframe old ones.

Design Thinking: A human-centered approach to problem-solving, Design Thinking combines empathy, experimentation, and prototyping to develop creative ideas. Used predominantly in product and service design, it can be applied broadly across various creative fields.

6.4. Harnessing Environments

Your surroundings play a crucial part in your creative journey. The right environment can spark creativity, while the wrong one may stifle it.

Nature: Numerous creators and thinkers have found inspiration in nature. The vast beauty, intricate details, and profound silence that nature offers can serve as a powerful catalyst to attract creative thoughts.

Changing Scenery: Venture beyond your usual work or play space. A change of scenery can break monotony and trigger novel perspectives. Cafes, libraries, museums or parks each offer a different atmosphere that can stimulate your creative thinking differently.

Organized Spaces: An organized workspace promotes a clear mind. Reduce clutter, categorize, and ensure every tool you need is at hand yet neatly arranged. The resulting serenity helps your mind focus and boosts your creative productivity.

Using the right tools and techniques to stimulate your creativity largely depends on personal exploration; what works for one may not work for another. Customizing these tools according to your requirements, style and comfort, and being consistent in their application, can greatly foster your creativity. Testing different approaches, being open to new ideas, and acknowledging that creative journeys are often non-linear helps your inner artist to flourish. Embrace the process, trust your instincts, let creativity flow and don't forget to have fun along the way. Creativity is as natural as it is rewarding, so enjoy the journey!

Chapter 7. Case Studies of Famous Creative Minds

Diving into the lives of creative geniuses, we unearth the keys that have unlocked the doors to their artistic intensity. These corridors lead to a realm of inspiration, that is as unending as it is fascinating. They serve not just as an insight into the workings of a mastermind, but also a blueprint of the journey towards creative confidence.

7.1. Pablo Picasso: The Versatile Visionary

Our first stop is at the colorful world of Pablo Picasso, an artist synonymous with innovation and audacity. Picasso, whose full name is thirteen-words long, was prolific in producing an estimated 50,000 artworks encompassing paintings, sculptures, ceramics, drawings, textiles, and even poetry. Throughout his career, he moved across various art styles like the Blue Period, Rose Period, African art-inspired Period, Cubism, Classicism, and Surrealism, thereby demonstrating his vast creative versatility.

Picasso was known to experiment with unconventional materials and techniques. He discovered his love of modeling while working in a ceramic shop in Paris, where he used discarded pieces and household objects to create unique sculptural forms. Picasso's zeal for exploration and his ability to turn the ordinary into the extraordinary are a testament to the power of creative confidence.

7.2. Emily Dickinson: The Reclusive Poetess

Next, we explore the world of Emily Dickinson, a poet who penned around 1800 poems, with less than a dozen published during her lifetime. Dickinson was known for her unconventional use of form and syntax - her works brimming with dashes, unconventional capitalizations, and short lines packed with meaning. Her creative genius often manifested in the familiar terrain of personal experiences, transforming the mundane into the magical.

The key takeaway from Dickinson's creative process is her introspective silence. Dickinson's choice of a largely reclusive life hints at the importance of solitude to nurture creativity, a stark contrast to Picasso's explorations. As Rainer Maria Rilke famously wrote, 'Love your solitude and try to sing out with the pain it causes you,' Dickinson's creative confidence shone in her explorations of the inner, quiet world.

7.3. Steve Jobs: The Design Innovator

Navigating the bylanes of creativity, we arrive at the intersection of technology and aesthetics in the persona of Steve Jobs. The co-founder of Apple, known for his impeccable sense of design and innovative products, Jobs transformed a garage-based startup into one of the most valuable companies on the planet. His visionary contributions include the Apple Macintosh, iPod, iPhone, and the iPad - all products that combined functionality with elegance.

Jobs' affinity for calligraphy during his college days influenced the typography in Apple computers, demonstrating the nexus between diverse interests. His belief, "Design is not just what it looks like and feels like. Design is how it works," underscores the integration of creativity and utility. Jobs' trajectory reveals that creative confidence often stems from the perfect blend of diligence, resilience, and daring to diverge from the norm.

7.4. Frida Kahlo: The Avatar of Self-Expression

In our quest, a significant detour directs us to the mesmerizing Frida Kahlo, an artist celebrated for her introspective self-portraits dripping with emotions. Facing numerous difficulties in life - from a crippling accident to tumultuous relationships - Kahlo used art as an outlet for her deepest sufferings. She boldly represented pain, identity, and feminine experience in her works, pioneering a unique blend of realism and symbolism.

Kahlo's creativity was deeply personal and, in many ways, therapeutic. Her creative confidence stemmed not from mastering technique, but her audacity to bare the deeply personal on canvas. Kahlo's story exemplifies the power of vulnerability in creativity and the strength that authenticity brings to artistic expression.

7.5. Conclusion

These formative examples serve as the stepping stones towards understanding our unique creative journeys. The beauty of creativity lies in its peculiar appeal; it is not a narrow path but a vast expanse that welcomes all. Whether it's Picasso's experimental curiosity, Dickinson's introspective solitude, Jobs' fusion of design and technology, or Kahlo's raw authenticity, the common thread is an unflinching belief in one's own creative potential - the bedrock of creative confidence.

As diverse these roads may appear, they share a common destination: a world painted bright with creativity. Every creative journey is steeped in courage - the courage to question, the courage to experiment, the courage to fail, and the courage to relentlessly pursue one's creative passion.

Chapter 8. Practical Exercises for Daily Creative Boost

Embracing creativity is akin to embracing exercise; your commitment to consistency is what cultivates growth and strength. In creativity, that means carving out time daily, even briefly, to engage in exercises designed to stretch your inventive muscles. Here, we offer a variety of exercises of varying intensities to cater to your energy levels throughout varying instances of the day.

Of course, like with physical exercise, the key to these practices lies not just in doing them, but in sincerely dedicating your presence to them. Muster the totality of your attention, ignore external distractions, and let the magic of creation unfold.

8.1. Morning Routine: Boost Your Creativity with Sunrise Simulations

Kickstart your day with a sunrise simulation. This exercise can involve anything, from sketching a sunrise to composing a morning melody or concocting a description of dawn's crack in a piece of prose. Morning time naturally stimulates creativity, and this exercise capitalizes on that concept.

The aim of this exercise is to embrace the day's new beginning, training yourself to see the beauty and potential that each fresh day offers. Remember: creativity thrives on optimism, and what could be more optimistic than the sun's daily rebirth?

8.2. Daily Art Challenges: Nurture Your Interest

Keeping the artistic spark alive requires feeding it with regular challenges. Choose a medium of your preference and take part in daily art challenges online. They often come with prompts that guide your day's theme. It forces you to think beyond your typical comfort zone, stretching your imagination while networking with other artists.

8.3. Mind-Mapping: The Web of Creative Thoughts

Mind-mapping is an excellent visual tool to explore the connectivity of ideas. Pick a random word or concept and note it in the center of a page. Now, start associating any ideas that come into your mind with this central notion, branching out the central idea into multiple strands of thought. You might be surprised by where your brain will take you!

8.4. Journaling: The Gateway to Self-discovery

Keeping a daily creative journal is one of the essential habits you can adopt to boost your creativity. Use it to record your thoughts, ideas, doodles, poems, or snapshots of your day. It's a personal space to explore yourself and your imagination, unjudged and unhindered. Moreover, looking back at your entries often sparks new ideas or brings a fresh perspective.

8.5. A Picture is Worth a Thousand Words

Choose a photograph from a magazine, newspaper, or the internet. Delve into recreating it in your way through drawing, writing, or collaging. The exercise aims to stimulate you to reinterpret and re-envision the world around you and train yourself to see the usual in unusual ways.

8.6. Object Redesign

Every day, find an ordinary object around you and redesign it on paper. Find ways to make it more beautiful, practical, or interesting. This hands-on exercise calls upon your critical thinking, challenging your status quo and offering creative solutions—a fundamental essence of creativity.

8.7. Embrace Boredom: Ideate from Nothingness

Boredom is contentious—it can be a blocker or an enhancer of creativity. Take 10-15 minutes to sit quietly, disconnect from all gadgets, and in this state of non-focused attention, jot down any ideas that emerge. These moments of disconnect often tap into deeper reservoirs of creativity and inspiration.

8.8. Innovation from Limitations

Create a spontaneous piece of art using three random items you find around you. This technique invokes creativity within constraints—a common situation in real-life creative problem-solving.

Remember, these exercises are meant to stimulate your creativity, not stress you out. Opt for ones that challenge but also excite you. Continue to switch exercises up, keeping your creative thinking on its toes. Persistence, patience, and an openness to exploring the curious realms of your psyche are vital ingredients for boosting your creativity. With this recipe in hand, go forth, and unleash the boundless potential of your imagination, every single day!

Chapter 9. Benefits of Creativity: A Broader Perspective

The roots of creativity dig deep into the fertile soil of human consciousness, sprouting remarkable ideas that shape societies, cultures, and individuals. Our lives are entwined with the strings of creativity, resonating with the beautiful melodies played by the maestro — the human mind. The benefits of creativity, in all its multifaceted glory, extend well beyond the confines of a canvas, a piece of music, or a meticulously crafted verse. The reach of its perennially branching roots encapsulate a broader perspective that encompasses the socio-personal, psychological, educational, and professional spheres of human existence.

9.1. The Socio-Personal Realm: Transforming Interactions and Experiences

Creativity is not limited to only those who identify as artists or innovators. It thrives within every human being, often influencing interactions and experiences in unforeseen ways. A creative approach enhances communication skills, lending a broader spectrum of expression that deepens interpersonal understanding.

Andy Warhol famously said, "They say that time changes things, but you actually have to change them yourself." Creativity equips individuals with the power to bring about change, not just in their lives but also in their communities. From community art projects to innovative social solutions, creativity is a catalyst for evolution, a tool that enables individuals to directly influence and improve their surroundings.

9.2. Empowerment through Emotional Release:

There is a strong interconnection between emotions and creativity. Throughout history, writers, painters, and musicians have used their craft as an outlet to express their emotions. Creating provides a sanctuary, an escape that allows us to confront our emotions without judgment or fear, and therein lies the power of healing.

Creativity allows an individual to gain control over their inner turmoil and share their feelings with the world through symbolic representations. It can help reduce anxiety, stress, and depression, making it not just a tool of self-expression but also a shield to guard one's mental health.

9.3. Educational Implications: Lighting the Flame of Learning

Fostering creativity in education can significantly enhance learning experiences. It encourages broader thought processes, equipping students with flexible thinking skills, fostering intellectual curiosity, and enhancing problem-solving abilities.

In an environment where traditional rote learning methods are increasingly losing their relevance, creativity-infused education has emerged as an essential tool to prepare young minds for an uncertain future. It strengthens metacognitive skills, educating individuals to think about how they think and learn. This plays a vital role in self-motivation and adaptability, facilitating personalised learning and the capacity to tackle novel situations.

9.4. Professional Benefits: The Creative Edge

Creativity is now one of the most sought-after skills in the professional sphere. It generates innovative solutions, improves the decision-making process, and aids the development of leadership skills by encouraging strategic thinking, resilience, and adaptability.

Robust creativity can be an invaluable asset that sets an individual apart in today's competitive job market. It promotes fluid and original thinking, enabling novel approaches to problem-solving, enhancing effectiveness in team collaborations, and generating economic growth through innovation.

9.5. Creativity: The Key to Self-Discovery and Personal Growth

Steering the searchlight internally, one of the most profound benefits of creativity is its role in personal growth and self-understanding. Creative expression offers a path to explore the complex labyrinth of personal identity, navigating experiences, perspectives, and emotions.

Embracing creativity can trigger an introspective journey of self-discovery — one where every stroke of the brush, every note played, or every word penned down offers an intimate interaction with the self.

9.6. In A Nutshell

The influence of creativity is not confined within the boundaries of artistic creation. Its benefits seep into our social and personal lives, enrich emailunications, empower emotional stability, light up learning experiences, and provide an edge in our professional pursuits. Embracing creativity bursts open the doors of self-discovery, leading to formidable personal growth. Its breadth of spectrum shows that it's not an elusive concept meant for a select few, but a universal phenomenon, deeply ingrained into the fabric of our being. It paints the canvas called 'life' in vibrant shades, highlighting the journey with moments of innovation, expansion, and fulfillment. It's time we unleash this boundless potential within, for creativity is not just about making things. It's about making things happen.

Chapter 10. Maintaining Consistency: Create Every Day

Creativity does not exist purely in spurts of inspiration. Like most things in life, it thrives on consistency. Every accomplished artist, author, or inventor has hours of committed work behind their success. They didn't rest on those rare moments when a stroke of genius hit them; instead, they made creating an integral part of their day, every day. This is the ultimate secret to nurturing your artistic genius actively, rather than passively waiting for inspiration to come knocking.

10.1. Harnessing the Power of Consistency

Consistency is the foundation of artistic prowess. Even the most gifted creators don't produce masterpieces every time they place pen to paper or brush to canvas. They commit to their craft and put in a substantial amount of work—regardless of the results. This commitment to consistent work helps them refine their abilities over time. They aren't born with an innate ability to create; instead, they learn how to channel their inspiration effectively through continued practice and dedication.

Building a daily ritual for creating can be a powerful tool for accelerating your journey towards artistic excellence. Such a ritual could involve, for instance, setting aside an hour every day solely for drawing, writing, sculpting, or whatever form your artistry takes. By fostering this habit, you subconsciously encourage your mind to traverse the labyrinth of creativity during that set period each day.

However, consistency is challenging to maintain. It demands motivation and a strong will to resist the alluring temptation to skip a day—especially on those days when you feel drained of inspiration.

10.2. Refrain from Pursuing Perfection

When Picasso said, "Every child is an artist; the problem is staying an artist when you grow up," he hit the nail on the head. As we age, we develop an obsession with perfection. We fear mistakes, imperfect results, and how others perceive our creations. Over time, this fear can morph into a formidable barrier inhibiting our creativity.

Shifting your perspective from pursuing perfection to embracing the process can essentially make a difference. See mistakes not as failures but as opportunities to learn and to grow. Your daily creative routine isn't about producing perfect works of art—it's about experimentation, self-expression, and enjoyment.

If you're writing a poem, don't worry about rhyming every line perfectly. If you're painting, free your hand to make strokes as they come naturally—don't stress about capturing every tiny detail. This isn't to say that you should neglect the quality of your work—but do not let the pursuit of perfect art stifle your creativity. It's more important to keep creating, learning, unlearning, relearning, and evolving each day.

10.3. Make Room for Creativity

Regardless of our chosen creative deliverance, we all need space where our ideas can take flight without being hindered by routine obligations or distractions. Much like an artist requires a studio, a writer needs a quiet corner to breathe life into words. Ensuring a designated creative space can greatly promote consistency.

This place could be anywhere—a room in your home, a corner of your favorite cafe, a peaceful outdoor spot. Make it your sanctum where you can unplug from your daily life, immerse in your thoughts, and channel your creative energy.

Furnishing this space with elements you love—be it an abundance of plants, inspiring art pieces, or a particular style of decor—can also enhance its ability to stimulate your imagination. Moreover, having your tools and materials within easy reach can make it easier to get started each day.

10.4. Develop Your Personal Creative Routine

Every creator has a unique routine that works best for them. Some might prefer the tranquil early mornings when the world is still asleep and your thoughts can flow freely. Some might resonate more with the peaceful solitude of the night. Experiment with different routines to discover the one that unleashes your maximum creativity.

It can be helpful to introduce specific cues into your routine that can signal to your brain that it's time to create. For instance, you could start each session by brewing a cup of coffee, going for a short walk, or playing your favorite soundtrack.

The idea is to let your brain associate these cues with your creative time, so even on days when you're feeling uninspired, these cues can help elicit the precise state of focus you need.

10.5. Note Down All Your Ideas

Remember, your every thought is valuable in the creative process, so it's essential to keep an idea journal. Despite your creative routine, inspiration can strike you anytime, anywhere. It could be while on a commute, in the middle of a conversation, or when listening to a piece of music.

Use a notebook or an app on your phone to jot down these ideas, no matter how insignificant they may seem at the moment. These fleeting thoughts can add unexpected dimensions to your creations later.

10.6. Embrace Slow Progress

Understand that becoming proficient at your preferred form of art will not occur overnight. You might not see considerable improvement quickly, but that surely doesn't mean you are not progressing.

Often, it's only when we look back at our past works after a considerable period that we can truly gauge how far we've come. Remember, the journey of creativity is a marathon, not a sprint—enjoy each step!

Getting into the habit of creating every day is an exciting but challenging endeavor—it's a journey filled with highs and lows, triumphs, and learning opportunities. Embrace this exciting process and let it guide you deeper into a rendezvous with your creative self. And remember, each day holds the promise of a new canvas—you only need to pick up the brush and start to paint.

Chapter 11. Cultivating A Life of Art: Your Creative Journey Starts Here

Art is everywhere. It's in the way the light streams through your window in the morning, it's in the melody of the birds' morning chorus. Art is in the universal language of a smile, the silent whisper of a falling leaf, and the vibrancy of your favorite color. It's in the stories that make us laugh, dream, and even question. Yet, it is often mistaken as an exclusive domain of those with exceptional talent. What we fail to grasp is the inherent artistry in every one of us. To actualize this artistry, we need to cultivate a life of art, embedding creativity in every living moment.

11.1. Embracing Your Individuality

First and foremost, recognize that your creative expression is as unique as your fingerprint. No one else can write your poem, paint your landscape or compose your melody. Find what resonates with you, what moves you, and let that be the primary fuel for your creative journey. Do not be disheartened if your work doesn't resemble the established norms of 'good' or 'successful' art. Embrace the idea that your art is an extension of yourself - it can be nothing but original and unique.

11.2. Inviting Inspiration

Inspiration is transient. Its fleeting nature often makes it elusive, but one thing is certain – inspiration loves an active mind. Read widely, learn voraciously and engage with different environments to keep your mind active and your inspiration flowing. Be aware of your surroundings, the sights, sounds, scents — art lives in the details that exist around you. Keep an open mind, for inspiration can peep from the most unlikely corners.

11.3. Cultivating Concentration

Art thrives in the realm of focus. Cultivate your ability to concentrate by practicing mindfulness. Pay attention to your thoughts, feelings, and sensation. The more perceptive you are, the deeper you can delve into your art. Consider devoting regular, undisturbed periods for indulging in your art. Create a personal sanctuary where your creativity can unfold without interruptions.

11.4. Embracing the Artistic Mindset

Artists are not made; they're self-born through an incessant journey of self-discovery and relentless practice. Expressing yourself artistically means embracing uncertainty, welcoming the unexpected and meeting failures with grace. Let go of your preoccupation with perfection because art is more about the process than the final product. Treat every artistic attempt as a step forward on this journey.

11.5. Nurturing Artistic Skills

Identify the skills that your art form requires and set about enhancing them. Be patient and persistent in your efforts. Practice, practice, and practice. But remember, true artistry transcends skill – it's your soul manifesting through your work. Hence, while technical skills are critical, don't let them take precedence over self-expression.

11.6. Appreciating Art

To create art, learn to appreciate it in every form. Spend time in galleries, listen to music across genres, read diverse literatures, watch a variety of films. Broaden your artistic palette, while absorbing and learning from the works of others. By appreciating others' art, you become more attuned to your own.

11.7. The Art of Living

Finally, art is not just about painting, sculpting, writing or composing music. It is a way of life. It's about transforming ordinary experiences into extraordinary ones, infusing mundanity with vibrance, and perceiving the world in your own unique way. Dedicate your whole life to the pursuit of this art.

To conclude, cultivating a life of art is a journey that extends beyond techniques, rules, or formulas. It is a continual process of self-discovery, self-expression, and constant learning. As you journey on this path, comprehend that every step is an achievement, every stumble an opportunity, and each moment a piece of art waiting to be created. Your creative journey starts here, not with a brush or a pen, but with your open heart and your wandering mind.